THE GUILDFORD HOME GUARD

S Y
4
INVISIBILITY

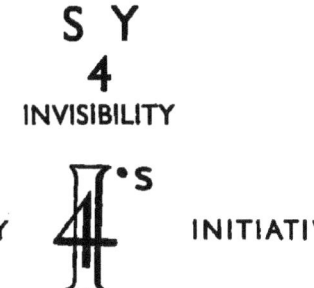

INDIVIDUALITY   INITIATIVE

INAUDIBILITY

18TH MAY 1940—31ST DECEMBER 1944

The Naval & Military Press Ltd

Published by

The Naval & Military Press Ltd
Unit 5 Riverside, Brambleside
Bellbrook Industrial Estate
Uckfield, East Sussex
TN22 1QQ England

Tel: +44 (0)1825 749494

www.naval-military-press.com
www.nmarchive.com

In reprinting in facsimile from the original, any imperfections are inevitably reproduced and the quality may fall short of modern type and cartographic standards.

FOREWORD

IN MY ATTEMPT TO WRITE AN ABRIDGED History of the 4th Guildford Battalion Surrey Home Guard, I am fully aware of the fact that I shall fall far short of painting a picture, as it should be painted, of the activities—the comings and goings of those Gallant Gentlemen of the L.D.V., who in the early days of 1940, when their country was in mortal danger, so splendidly answered the call to arms in order to defend the homeland. It was assuredly they who made the Guildford Battalion of the Home Guard second to none—nor can I pay sufficient tribute to those who joined later.

Only those in intimate touch, as I was privileged to be, knew and realized what these Gallant Gentlemen did; indeed, they can aptly be termed "The Gallant Endeavours." Theirs, indeed, was a moral obligation voluntarily performed with credit, and worthily did they, in their small way, play their part in upholding the great traditions of the Queen's Royal Regiment

PRISTINÆ VIRTUTIS MEMOR

G. W. Geddes

D DAY, 1944

[Photo: W. Dennett, Guildford

4th GUILDFORD BATTALION SURREY HOME GUARD

THE 4th Guildford Battalion Surrey Home Guard was raised by Colonel G. W. Geddes on the 18th May, 1940, on which date some 300 citizens of Guildford reported at 1400 hours at the headquarters of the Surrey Constabulary in Guildford for enrolment in the L.D.V.

The peril of those days—the prospect of imminent invasion and national danger—was such that an immediate decision had to be made as to how best to organize and administer those early volunteers called the L.D.V.

There was nothing to build on except improvization, and those who had previously served in the Services were in a minority.

On the principle of local defence the Battalion Area of Responsibility was divided into areas, or cantons, of defence, so that those citizens living in their respective areas should be banded together, each in his own commando. This had the advantage of having volunteers serving in areas intimately known to them and the personal touch of actually defending their own hearths and homes.

The Battalion Area of Responsibility was that contained within the Borough of Guildford boundary, a circumference of some twenty-five miles.

The Battalion was then organized into twelve Platoon Areas.

Such an organization was simple and facilitated administration, besides being tactically sound, and followed the principle and example of organizations adopted by the Territorial Army in the United Kingdom and countries of the Continent.

This co-ordination welded the Battalion together into a homogeneous whole, producing great *esprit de corps* and the keenness of rivalry between the companies into which the Battalion was eventually organized.

As could only be expected, the Battalion started from zero. There was no organization or cadre on which to build and there was no likelihood, in those days, of any outside help. The Battalion had to stand on its own feet. There were no arms, no equipment, no uniforms, nor was there any information as to when or how arms would be issued or in what quantity. All that was known was that the country was in a state of national danger and imminent invasion.

As Guildford was a reception area its population had been doubled, with the result that there was no accommodation for any Headquarters. All barracks were occupied by the Army. In consequence, improvization was the order of the day.

Owners of private houses responded patriotically by giving up their garages and, in some cases, rooms in their homes as headquarters for platoons. Battalion Headquarters was in a private house in full occupation.

To this there was an exception. The Surrey County Council gracefully handed over Henley Fort for the use of the L.D.V. This made an ideal headquarters in every way, both tactically and administratively. It was in a most important sector of Guildford, and from the 18th May, 1940, to the 31st December, 1944, was the Headquarters of what was eventually "E" Company of the Battalion.

Great credit must be given to the Guildford Borough Police in those early days for the great assistance they gave in the enrolment of volunteers at their Headquarters in North Street, and in permitting them to be used as an arsenal for the safe custody of arms and ammunition when delivered, before distribution could be made.

What appeared to be insuperable difficulties were overcome by the untiring energy and will to do of those early volunteers who gave so freely of their spare time to make good. Theirs is the credit.

Everyone of those volunteers was fully employed in his civilian capacity; and yet, after a hard day's toil, they all devoted night after night, for months and years on end, in the administration of their commands and by training to make themselves as best they could into a force to be reckoned with.

At the start the Battalion was organized into platoons, platoons of a strength of 100 or more other ranks. Commanders of platoons were selected and appointed from a list submitted by the Police of citizens of Guildford known for their integrity and standing. These citizens were appointed to command in those sectors or wards in which they lived. This had the advantage that they knew the other citizens living in their own part of the Borough and made, in consequence, the selection of N.C.Os. by them easier than had it been otherwise.

On the 19th May, 1940, 150 Ross rifles were issued with 20 rounds of S.A.A., besides shot-guns which local citizens generously gave. An even distribution was made.

On the night of the 19th-20th May the Guildford L.D.V. was ON DUTY !

On the 19th May the first Battalion conference was held, and commanders were given the Areas of Responsibility of their commands.

Time was short indeed in those early days if the Battalion was to be a factor in the defence of the country. An immediate decision had, therefore, to be made as to the quickest and best method on which to train civilians and turn them into a fighting force, and, further, to decide on the operational role best suited for this untrained citizen force of volunteers.

The only directive received was "to defend the Area of Responsibility of the Battalion."

It was therefore decided that the Battalion, as it was constituted, could do no better than model itself on the lines of other citizen forces such as the Boers of South African War days, the tribesmen of the North West Frontier of India, and the partisans—in fact, become adepts at guerrilla warfare, because it was quite rightly realized that there was not the time to train on the lines of the Regular soldier, nor was it possible to have the ability to combat in the encounter battle an enemy superbly trained, led and armed.

Instructions issued by Battalion Headquarters on the policy to be adopted in training.

Ability to use the rifle; a thorough knowledge of the country by night as well as by day; fieldcraft and camouflage. These, it was decided, were the main essentials on which to build up the Battalion as a fighting force. On these lines of training the Battalion motto of the four I's was chosen:—

> Invisibility.
> Inaudibility.
> Individuality.
> Initiative.

This motto was proudly displayed in every headquarters. Simple as it was, it proved itself an invaluable guide and directive.

From the very start it was fully realized that it was imperative to obtain good officers and N.C.O. instructors with as little delay as possible, and thus it was that every vacancy offered on courses of instruction was avidly seized on and every channel explored from which help could be given. The willingness, keenness and desire of the volunteers in this Battalion to attend every and any course paid in the end handsome dividends, and before very long the Battalion possessed some first-class instructors in every weapon with which the Battalion was armed.

In those early days the defence of Guildford Town proper was the operational role of the Queen's I.T.C. and other Regular troops. The Battalion operated in close co-operation on the outer perimeter, by defending the road blocks at the approaches to Guildford, besides covering and observing all roads and areas of the Borough boundary on which an enemy might advance.

Operational Instruction No. 1 was issued at a Conference on Monday, 27th May, 1940. This was the first of the Monday night conferences held weekly for officers for four and a half years at which orders, instructions, training, tactics, operational and administrative problems were discussed and studied. These conferences proved invaluable and resulted in the Battalion being a homogeneous whole.

These instructions were based on the first instructions issued by Dorking Sub-District, under whose command the Battalion served. They substantiated in detail the instructions given during the week to commanders as to Areas of Responsibility and the action to be taken by all companies.

From July, 1940, picquets of a strength of 30 other ranks were mounted by companies daily from sunset to sunrise, and were operative until December, 1942, when it was considered by the Higher Command that the general situation had rendered these picquets no longer necessary. An excellent system was devised for "call up" should the occasion arise, and inlying picquets were detailed at a moment's call as long as the Battalion was in being.

1940

June 1st, 1940.	Guards were mounted at all the Borough waterworks.
June 14th, 1940.	L.D.V. armlets were issued.
July 6th, 1940.	The first denim uniform and F.S. caps were issued.

A fresh organization was ordered and companies came into being.

Group organizers became officially Battalion Commanders.

Platoon commanders became Company Commanders.

Section leaders became Platoon Commanders.

July 17th, 1940	420 P.14 S.M.L.E. rifles and 20 rounds of S.A.A. per rifle were received.
July 18th, 1940.	Mr. Charles Hirst, M.C., was appointed Administrative Assistant to the Battalion, he and the Commanding Officer representing Battalion Headquarters.
July 31st, 1940.	The strength of the Battalion had risen to 850 volunteers, armed with 450 rifles and shot guns. Captain C. H. Frisby was appointed Second-in-Command. The Battalion now took on a further operational commitment, and it was held responsible for the defence of the G.H.Q. Stopline within the limits of the Borough boundary.
August, 1940.	The P.14 S.M.L.E. rifles issued to the Battalion were withdrawn and the Battalion was re-armed with 700 .300 Springfield rifles with 40 rounds of S.A.A. per rifle. Twelve Browning automatic rifles were also issued—a first-class weapon when used as a single shot arm and discharged in a static position.
August 7th, 1940.	Battalion Headquarters was established in two rooms at the Borough Hall. During August, platoons in the Battalion became affiliated to various National Rifle Clubs at Bisley, and the first practice with ball ammunition took place on Bisley Range, ammunition having been purchased privately to the extent of 10,000 rounds of S.A.A. In fact, one platoon had devoted every weekend at Bisley since early June.

To assist the Police, traffic control was added to the duties of the Battalion. The end of the year saw the Battalion well established as a fighting unit. Much hard work had been done. Training had been consistent and progressive. The syllabus of training was laid down by Battalion Headquarters and strictly adhered to.

Every night instruction in the rifle, patrols and fieldcraft was given, patrols going out in Platoon Areas of Responsibility. Sundays were devoted to small platoon or inter-platoon exercises.

October, 1940.
The first issue of greatcoats was made, an article of clothing very much required. Something definite had been accomplished. The strength of the Battalion had risen to approximately 1,800 all ranks.

1941

January, 1941.
An Intelligence Section was formed under Lieut. A. Smith. Small beginnings lead to greater things, the Intelligence Section providing the personnel at Battalion H.Q. for Operational H.Q. It achieved a very high state of efficiency. On the many District and Sub-District and Battalion exercises of from twelve to eighteen hours' duration it carried out its duties in a highly efficient manner.

January 2nd, 1941.
The first issue of serge battledress, steel helmets, haversacks and more greatcoats was made. C.S.M. Flower, of the East Surreys, reported for duty as P.S.I. to the Battalion. Immediately courses of instruction were started at Battalion H.Q., and as further weapons were issued so each company sent N.C.Os. to attend the Battalion courses of instruction.

February 2nd, 1941.	A much needed addition in arms was received in the shape of two .300 Vickers machine guns.
February 18th, 1941.	Four Browning medium machine guns were issued. The lack of light automatics was of great consequence, and a wish never satisfied. It was felt that the issue of Bren guns was a vital need. Box respirators were issued.
March 1941.	A further issue of greatcoats, which were badly needed. The first anti-tank weapon, the Northover projector, was issued. Serge battledress was issued to the Battalion and the denim uniform returned to store.
April, 1941.	An issue of twelve Thompson sub-machine guns was made. These were eventually withdrawn, being required for the Army. Commissions were granted to the Home Guard.
June, 1941.	The Battalion was reorganized into six General Duty companies and one Factory Guard company as follows:—

Battalion Headquarters:

Commanding Officer	Lieut.-Colonel G. W. Geddes, D.S.O.
Second-in-Command	Major C. H. Frisby, V.C.
Intelligence and Liaison Officer	Lieut A. Smith.
Ammunition Officer	Captain G. Vincent.
Administrative Assistant ...	Mr. C. H. Hirst, M.C.
"A" Coy. Commander	Major G. Stafford.
"B" Coy. Commander	Major R. W. Black.
"C" Coy. Commander	Major C. R. Wigan, M.C.,T.D.,D.L.
"D" Coy. Commander	Major L. Edge.
"E" Coy. Commander	Major G. L. Batrum.
"F" Coy. Commander	Major W. G. Sheppard.
"G" Coy. Commander	Major C. T. Skipper.

June 16th, 1941.	On the reorganization of the Battalion, Lieut.-Colonel H. C. Theobald, D.S.O., who raised the original "C" Company, tendered his resignation and Major L. Edge assumed command in December.
July, 1941.	The first weapon training course was held at Westcott and Bisley Ranges. The course was based on the Weapon Training Course as laid down for the Army in pre-war days for classification. Great keenness was shown and 92 per cent. of the Battalion were exercised. Thanks to practices at Bisley with affiliated Rifle Clubs, the results were of quite a high standard.
July 6th, 1941.	The Battalion was inspected by the Zone Commander, Major-General A. P. Y. Langhorne, C.B., D.S.O., M.C.
August 15th, 1941.	The I.T.C. of the Queen's Royal Regiment moved out and the defence of Guildford as an "A" Nodal Point became the responsibility of the Battalion. Home Guard flashes and titles were issued to the Battalion, and the old Home Guard brassards which had replaced the L.D.V. brassards were withdrawn.
November, 1941.	The definite defensive perimeter of the Guildford nodal point was decided on and, very shortly afterwards, work on the anti-tank ditches, road blocks and wiring commenced. The nodal point was divided into five sectors of defence and areas of responsibility allocated to "A," "B," "C," "D" and "F" Companies, "E" Company being held in general reserve.
December, 1941.	1,000 rifles and bayonets had been issued to the Battalion. The Battalion was affiliated to a battalion of the Lancashire Fusiliers for a week only, owing to the exigencies of the Service.

To recapitulate all that had taken place and been done in training would take too long, and space does not permit. The Battalion had made immense strides towards efficiency. Apart from training on week days and at nights, companies devoted at least two Sundays a month to small tactical exercises. Exercises were held by District and Sub-District to test communications and the rapidity with which the Battalion could be at "action stations." In addition, exercises were set by Battalion Headquarters and Exercise "Action Stations" held on five occasions. The average number of those turning out within two hours was a very high percentage.

1942

January 25th, 1942.	A large-scale "Action Station" exercise was held.
	Operational duties on picquets had become heavy, and the average of nights in bed was one in five.
February, 1942.	Billeting arrangements and feeding within the nodal point for action stations were completed.
March, 1942.	The first issue of Spigot mortars was made to the Battalion, and eventually twenty-four were issued. Teams were trained and carefully sighted emplacements constructed for the static defence of the nodal point.
April, 1942.	The Battalion was affiliated to the Seaforth Highlanders for a negligible duration of time. The chief item of instruction given was street fighting.
	A further allotment of L.M.Gs. was made to the Battalion, consisting of six .303 Vickers machine guns and two Browning machine guns. The issue of machine guns was eventually increased so that the Battalion had sixteen Vickers and two Browning machine guns. All these machine guns were in fixed positions in carefully constructed emplacements on the perimeter of the nodal

point. A carefully co-ordinated fire plan was drawn up in conjunction with the Smith guns, Spigot mortars and small arms.

May, 1942.
A big "Action Stations" exercise was held by the Battalion, incorporating personnel of the A.T.S. from Stoughton Camp. May, 1942, was indeed a busy month for the Battalion.

Exercises to test the ability of the Battalion to man action stations were held on the 6th, the 14th, the 16th and the 25th. On the 16th the enemy was represented by a young soldier battalion of The East Surrey Regiment. The clash of arms had its amusing side. These young soldiers, overcome with keenness and excitement, were somewhat contemptuous of the old gentlemen of the Home Guard, and thought they could be pushed aside. Their ardour was somewhat damped by the Home Guard exhibiting a considerable knowledge of unarmed combat, in which a good number had been put through. That on the 16th was set by the District Commander, who, at his conference on the 20th, complimented in no mean terms the efficiency of the Battalion and the turn-out, 93 per cent. of the Battalion participating.

The Battalion was informed that there would be no .300 ammunition available to fire weapon training courses with the Springfield rifles with which it was armed. But this did not deter the Battalion from firing a weapon training course with borrowed S.M.L.E. rifles.

June, 1942.
Another busy month for the Battalion. The Spider system of communication within the nodal point was completed, and a Battalion "Action Stations" exercise held to test out the system. Nodal point, Battalion and No.

5 Sector H.Q. were well tested, some 340 messages passing through by phone and runner.

The Battalion was affiliated to the Toronto Scottish for what was termed an "Army Fortnight." Too high praise cannot be given to this magnificent Regiment for their co-operation, willingness to teach and enter into everything. Being a Machine Gun Battalion, their *raison d'etre* was the machine gun, and every advantage was taken on normal nights of training to have machine-gun teams trained by them. Despite the fact that the Toronto Scottish was primarily an M.G. battalion, their versatility was such that they entered wholeheartedly into the scheme of things to act as enemy airborne troops. Each company of the Battalion had one night exercise a week and two large-scale Battalion exercises were held on the 13th-14th and 20th-21st. The officers of the Toronto Scottish attended the weekly conference for officers of the Battalion, and a great spirit of *camaraderie* existed.

June also saw the commencement of battle innoculation on the Battalion bombing range on Guildown. Machine guns of the Toronto Scottish operated at first, but eventually battle innoculation was carried out by the machine guns of the Battalion.

June 24th, 1942.	Mr. Charles Hirst resigned his appointment as Administrative Assistant to the Battalion, to which he had given yeoman service.
	C.Q.M.S. Bryant of the Queen's Royal Regiment carried out these duties till December.
July and August, 1942.	Tactical Camps of Training were held, where the men lived hard. These were much enjoyed and instructive training was carried out.

August, 1942.	The first issue of Sten guns to the Battalion.

A Transport Section was formed under Lieut. Jennings and commanded by 2/Lieut. C. W. Levinge. This Transport Section, with commercial vehicles earmarked by local tradesmen, was always to the fore when tactical exercises were held and were very efficient.

This month also saw the directing of compulsorily enlisted men into the Home Guard, many of whom, prevented for some reason or another from voluntarily enlisting, proved themselves to be of great worth. |
| September 14th, 1942. | Captain R. Turgel, of "F" Company of the Battalion, was appointed Adjutant, receiving a commission in the Officers' War Reserve. A further issue of .300 ammunition for the Springfield rifles, with which the Battalion was armed, enabled the Battalion to fire a second weapon training course, and it was gratifying to see the large number of those who were exercised and the high standard attained. |
| October, 1942. | A weapon training course was fired by the machine guns and Browning automatic rifles. The dark evenings of the autumn saw great activity by companies in small night exercises. |
| November, 1942. | A programme of individual training for the winter months was circulated to all companies to deal chiefly with the compulsorily enlisted men. By now the Battalion possessed good instructors. Subjects and details for proficiency test examinations of a very high standard were drawn up. The standard set was a great deal higher than that officially laid down.

The ceiling strength of the Battalion was 2,700, and this was reached by the end of 1942. |

December, 1942.	This month saw a keenly felt want met in the shape of Nissen huts for company stores. These were built at Lea Pale Lane Barracks.

1942 closed as a year of great endeavour. Much had been attempted and much accomplished. It was indeed a year that could be looked back on with satisfaction. Guards and picquets were new considered to be unnecessary by the Higher Command and ceased to mount, each company instead having an inlying platoon ready at a moment's call.

1943

March, 1943.	The Battalion was issued with Smith guns, a weapon which was most popular in the Battalion, and a quite high degree of proficiency was attained with live shell up to a range of 500 yards, some gun teams attaining a standard of indirect fire.
March and 1943.	Proficiency test examinations were held. The examining officers and instructor N.C.Os. from one company examining candidates presenting themselves from other companies. Great keenness was shown and a large number presented themselves for examination.
April, 1943.	Training, based on a syllabus from Battalion H.Q., commenced in April and was progressive for section, platoon, company and Battalion training.
May, 1943.	A further issue of Sten guns to the Battalion. A Battalion cadre course for N.C.O. instructors was held immediately by the P.S.I.
May 16th, 1943.	To celebrate the anniversary of the raising of the Home Guard a ceremonial parade was held in Shalford Flats. Sir Malcolm Fraser, Bart., G.B.E., the Lord-Lieutenant of the County of Surrey, graciously consented to inspect the Battalion as reviewing officer. After marching past, the Battalion gave a demonstration of the weapons with which

it was armed—machine guns, Spigot mortars and Northovers, engaging a tank with marked success. A very large crowd of onlookers was present, and the parade was a decided success. Major C. H. Frisby, V.C., Second-in-Command of the Battalion, broadcast an excellent commentary on the items carried out. The Battalion was highly complimented by the Lord-Lieutenant and the Commander of the Surrey and Sussex District. A more beautiful setting or a more perfect day for the parade could not have been wished for. It having been found impossible to obtain a band for the parade, the Drums of the Coldstream Guards, by kind permission of Colonel M. Trew, Lieutenant-Colonel commanding the Regiment, paraded with the Battalion and played the Battalion past the reviewing officer.

June, 1943.	At the request of the Regional Commissioner for Civil Defence, the Battalion sent a quota of men to be trained in Rescue Party and Trailer pump duties, and by September was manning two Rescue Party teams and two Trailer Pump teams nightly.
June 16th, 1943.	Major H. G. Stafford resigned and handed over the command of "A" Company to Major A. D. Crosby, M.B.E. Major L. Edge, who had commanded "D" Company for two years, gave up command of the company on joining the Regular Army.
July 18th, 1943.	"E" Company furnished a party of 34 other ranks to represent German paratroops in an exercise, set by the Sub-District Commander, to raid Chilworth Station and destroy the bridge, signal box and sidings. This task was successfully accomplished before the Home Guard responsible for that area were aware of the fact, creating alarm and

	despondency with confusion to the Company Commander in the midst of a cross-word puzzle. The commander of the Sub-District under-estimated the speed with which Home Guards could, when put to it, travel five miles across difficult country. He had aptly named the exercise "Dash."
July and August, 1943.	Tactical camps were held as in 1942.
August, 1943.	Major W. G. Sheppard, who had raised and commanded the company since May, 1940, voluntarily resigned to join the Regular Forces, handing over command of "F" Company to Major O. Crawt. "F" Company was then 450 strong.
September, 1943.	The travelling wing from the Home Guard W.T. School visited the Battalion to instruct officers and N.C.O. instructors in the rifle, grenades, Sten guns, Spigot mortars and Smith guns. The attendance was 100 per cent. during the week and the Battalion received an excellent report.
September and October, 1943.	The Battalion fired its fourth weapon training course with the rifle. Machine gun teams and Browning automatic rifles also fired a course, the latter at Westcott Range. Excellent results were obtained in all weapons.
November 21st, 1943.	An ambitious and well-executed field firing scheme for machine guns was fired at Westcott Range by six machine-gun teams of "A" Company. The District Commander was present and complimented the Company on their excellent fire control and shooting.
November, 1943.	Fourteen Rescue Party and Trailer Pump teams had been trained.

December 5th, 1943.   The G.O.C.-in-C. Home Forces was present for a while to watch a large-scale Battalion exercise in which "A," "E" and "F" Companies participated.

In 1943 the Battalion had attained a strength of 3,200 other ranks and was well armed with small arms, machine guns, Smith guns and Spigot mortars. 1943 saw another year of strenuous endeavour pass. The time had now come, after three years of hard training, to reduce the hours of training.

Practice "Action Stations" exercises for the Battalion were held on five occasions, and the keen response made was shown by the high percentage of men reporting on parade.

Each company now had a large percentage of men trained in handling the 36 Mills grenade. The Battalion bombing range had more than justified the expense involved, not only for instruction in live grenade throwing, but also for instruction in the rifle, Sten and machine guns, for which it was largely used.

1944

Training in the early months of the year was confined to instruction in the Smith gun, the Spigot mortar, machine guns and small night exercises.

January, 1944.   Major G. Batrum, who had commanded "E" Company from June, 1940, resigned from the Home Guard and transferred his activities to mountain warfare at the request of the War Office, where his knowledge, as a member of the Alpine Club, of mountaineering and how to live hard in mountain regions was sought in the formation and training of this new branch of the Service.

Captain P. J. Spooner, the second-in-command of the Company, took over command.

Major M. P. Bevan also assumed command of "D" Company.

February 5th, 1944.   A big communications exercise, as for "Action Stations" was held.

March 19th, 1944   The biggest practice "Action Stations" exercise was held, which was chiefly concerned with administration and the issuing of ammunition for all weapons down to rifles and Sten guns from company magazines to the actual men at their positions on the perimeter of the Nodal Point and all battle sections in their action station areas outside the perimeter. Although this was a twenty-four hour exercise, it was of the greatest value. As it proved a thorough test of organization and administration in the supply of ammunition from Battalion and company magazines as for action stations, it helped inordinately to rectify faults and speed up distribution. The Transport Section was fully up to their duties, which they performed with great credit. Number reporting for duty was 82 per cent.

April 21st, 1944. The Battalion was ordered to find a guard for the Chalk Tunnel. The first guard was supplied by "E" Company, and so keen was the spirit of the men that double the number required reported for duty. Strength of guard: 1 Sergeant, 2 Corporals and 16 men. No protective defensive wire entanglements existed, so from the first night on duty companies sent down wiring parties to wire up a defensive area. A defence scheme was drawn up, and all guards coming on duty were exercised in their role. Major C. H. Frisby, V.C., supervised the work of the wiring parties each and every night. Transport was provided to bring guards from their various company assembly points to their guard and return them on completion of their duty, otherwise they could not have got back in time for their daily work. The Battalion H.Q. was manned on a twenty-four hour basis.

April 23rd, 1944. The first "sitrep" was sent out at 0400 hours, and then daily at 1600 and 0400 hours.

April 28th, 1944.	A "Bugbear Action Stations" was ordered by G.O.C. Southern Command. Messages were quickly got to all Company Commanders and Company Headquarters, which were all manned. The Spider system of communication within the Nodal Point operated at under two hours. This, the Battalion was informed, was the final test. The Battalion was complimented on the rapidity with which it went to action stations. No indication had been given that this exercise was to be held, and it came as a complete surprise, which greatly enhanced its value to the Battalion as a test. Many thought that it was at last "Action Stations." In this connection an instance occurred which was typical of the spirit permeating the Battalion. "D" Company were enjoying a convivial gathering at a well-known local hostelry at which the Company Commander was present. It was only natural for all ranks to be upset and think it was most inconsiderate of Battalion H.Q. to order "Bugbear Action Stations." True to the traditions of the Battalion, the Company forgot their grievance and rushed to arms. Battalion H.Q. were forgiven.
March and April, 1944.	Examination of candidates in proficiency tests. Many candidates obtained their second Proficiency Test Badge.
June 4th, 1944.	To start the Soldiers' Week in Guildford the Battalion staged a miniature Aldershot Tattoo on Shalford Flats, at which the Secretary of State for War, Sir James Grigg, was present as reviewing officer. The Battalion was inspected and marched past, and the following demonstrations given:—

    (i) Rescue Party teams demonstrated with their lorries how to get casualties out of a bombed house (which had been erected for the purpose by the Borough Engineer).

(ii) Trailer Pump teams came into action and demonstrated how to put a fire out in the burning house.

(iii) Machine guns gave a display of coming into action.

(iv) Smith guns came into action with live shells, engaging moving tanks cleverly designed by the Borough Engineers and, by an ingenious method of rails and pulleys, designed by Lieut. Norman Harris, M.M., of "E" Company.

(v) The "Battle of Guildford." In which Home Guards disguised in the uniform of German airborne troops attacked a perimeter line held by Home Guards. They were counterattacked by battle sections of "E," "F," "C" and "D" Companies, the object of this part of the demonstration being to show the action taken by the battle sections and their role.

(vi) The Finale. The Battalion formed up in line, with Rescue Party and Trailer Pump teams on the right, and with machine guns and Smith guns on the left flank. The Battalion presented arms. God save the King.

The Band of the 30th Queen's, by kind permission of the Commanding Officer, played the Battalion by in the march past and gave a selection of music during the display.

Major C. H. Frisby, V.C., Second-in-Command of the Battalion, broadcast an excellent commentary, describing in simple terms all the demonstrations taking place. This was much appreciated by the spectators and clearly heard over this large arena by everyone.

The Lord Lieutenant, Sir Malcolm Fraser, Bart., G.B.E., the G.O.C. Southern Command, the Commander of Kent and Surrey Districts, the Sub-District commanders, the Mayor and Corporation were among the many distinguished visitors to honour the Tattoo with their presence. The Battalion received many congratulatory and complimentary messages from the Higher Command for the display it had given.

June 6th, 1944.
D Day.
The 30th Queen's relieved the Battalion guard on the Chalk Tunnel. The Battalion was ordered to take over the Sand Tunnel guard and mounted a guard of one Sergeant and 28 other ranks.

Here, again, no attempt had been made previously to put this vital area in a state of defence. A very large and ambitious wiring scheme was laid on and the whole area was eventually wired in with a double apron fence and triple Dannert. Every night large parties were detailed for wiring duties under the able guidance of the Second-in-Command, Major C. H. Frisby, V.C., who was indefatigable, as was his wont.

A well-considered defence scheme was drawn up with which all officers were thoroughly conversant. Guards were practised at their action stations.

July 9th, 1944.
Amongst the many tactical camps an excellent camp at Hascombe was held and an ambitious exercise set by Major M. Bevan, commander of "D" Company. In his zeal for setting booby traps he met with a very serious accident and had to be rushed to hospital, from which he happily recovered in a short time from his wounds.

July 22nd, 1944.
A big-scale exercise was held from 1700 hours to 0630 hours 23rd July by the Battalion, in which paratroops of the U.S.A. acted as the enemy. They were most ably guided by Quisling officers of the Battalion. The exercise was indeed most realistic and instructive.

September 9th, 1944.	The Battalion stood down. Sand Tunnel guards and all company picquets were dismissed.
	During this time the Battalion fired its fifth Weapon Training course for rifles as well as W.T. courses for M.G. and B.A.Rs.
	It is worthy of record that Major C. R. Wigan, M.C., T.D., was the only Company Commander who commanded a company from start to finish in the life of the Battalion, and Major R. W. Black from the day the Battalion was organized into six general duty companies.
December 3rd, 1944.	The Battalion paraded for the last time in the Technical College grounds and was formed up in a hollow square. The Band of the Queen's Royal Regiment, by kind permission of the Commanding Officer, was in attendance. The number on parade was 1,200.
	The Battalion was under the command of Major C. H. Frisby, V.C., who handed it over to the Commanding Officer.
	After inspecting the Battalion the Commanding Officer said goodbye to the Battalion. In his address he paid high tribute to all ranks for the way they had acquitted themselves and never let up since the day they were raised on the 18th May, 1940, until this their last parade. Their discipline, integrity and *esprit de corps* was of a truth the corner stone on which the Battalion was built and made it second to none. The Battalion was indeed a team "All for one, and one for all." Their loyalty and goodwill to him throughout these long years of stress made his task as a Commanding Officer an easy and unforgettable one.
	The Battalion then marched past for the last time, the Commanding Officer taking the salute.

In the meantime the Battalion was busily engaged in handing in its arms and equipment. In a formation like a Home Guard battalion, with its members scattered all over Guildford, this was no easy task; but, thanks to the goodwill and *esprit de corps* that permeated the Battalion, the results achieved were magnificent and the deficiencies negligible—in fact, it might be said of four companies it was nil, and this after four years and eight months' service. Chief credit must go to Company Commanders and the C.Q.M.Ss., whose indefatigable efforts to achieve such results are deserving of the highest recognition. A special word of praise and thanks is due to the Battalion's Quartermaster, Captain A. Forbes, to whom the Battalion owes a great debt of thanks.

This simple story of the Battalion cannot be closed without paying tribute to those ladies who volunteered for secretarial work at Battalion and Company Headquarters. They always reported for duty as members of the Battalion (which they were) at the many practice "Action Stations" exercises held, as well as at the many exercises held by Captain Smith for instruction in operational duties at Battalion H.Q. Had the Battalion gone to "Action Stations" everyone knew that *they would be there and worthily play their part.*

December 31st, 1944.   The Battalion was disbanded. Strength, 1,887 all ranks.

1945

June 30th, 1945.   The final imprest account, vouchers, and all documents had been handed into the Surrey T.A. and A.F. Association.

It might well be said of the Battalion that something had been accomplished and something done. That high spirit of endeavour born on that memorable day, 18th May, 1940, never died and was there to the end of the chapter. No tribute is too high to pay to these great gentlemen of the 4th Guildford Battalion Surrey Home Guard.

In conclusion, it is fitting to put on record the average number of days of twenty-four hours put in on guards, picquets and training by those men who enrolled voluntarily in the early days. Few realize or know what was done. The figure is astounding!

On a computation of actual hours performed and spent on operational duty and training (hours turned into days) by this part-time unpaid Battalion of Home Guard the figure is truly amazing. The majority of the L.D.V. and first Home Guards put in 308 days, of which 78 days were on operational picquet duties and patrols, and a further 15 days guarding the lines of communication from the 21st April, 1944, to 9th September, 1944.

"Invisible, Inaudible, Individual, Initiative."

APPENDICES

✚

Appendix "A" THE FIRST LIST OF OFFICERS

Appendix "B" LIST OF OFFICERS AT STAND DOWN, 9TH SEPT., 1944

Appendix "C" THE DISPOSITION, STRENGTH AND WEAPONS OF THE BATTALION IN THE DEFENCE OF GUILDFORD NODAL POINT

Appendix "D" AWARDS FOR MERITORIOUS SERVICE

APPENDIX "A"

4TH GUILDFORD BATTALION SURREY HOME GUARD

6th July, 1940.

HEADQUARTERS: Borough Hall, Haydon Place, Guildford. Tel.: 1629.
COMMANDING OFFICER: Colonel G. W. Geddes, D.S.O., Riverdene, Warwicks Bench, Guildford. Tel.: 1225.
ADMINISTRATIVE ASSISTANT: Captain C. H. Hirst, M.C., Marigolds, Harvey Road, Guildford. Tel.: 3185.
INTELLIGENCE AND LIAISON OFFICER: Captain F. E. Lee, Mynthurst, Epsom Road, Guildford. Tel.: 187.

"A" COMPANY

COMPANY COMMANDER: Mr. H. G. Stafford, Bareilly, Tilehurst Estate. Tel.: 1543.
SECOND-IN-COMMAND: Mr. W. R. Palmer, 18, Weston Road, Guildford.

PLATOON	COMMANDER	ADDRESS	AREA OF RESPONSIBILITY	HEADQUARTERS
No. 1	Mr. W. E. Haggar	3, Hereford Close	Westborough and Stoughton, London and Aldershot railway lines inclusive.	Hull's Farm. Tel.: Worplesdon 121
No. 2	Mr. D. J. Morris	The Chalet, Johnston Walk, Tilehouse.		Ditto
No. 3	Mr. A. D. Crosby	Collingwood, Woking Road. Tel.: 2713.	Stoughton, Stoke Hill Park, Railway exclusive, River Wey inclusive.	Stoke Hill Farm. Tel.: 2456.

26

"B" Company

COMPANY COMMANDER: Colonel C. R. Wigan, M.C., T.D., D.L., Farthings, Longdown Road, Guildford. Tel.: 1450.

SECOND-IN-COMMAND: Captain E. H. Shepard, M.C., Long Meadow, Longdown Road, Guildford. Tel.: 1607.

PLATOON	COMMANDER	ADDRESS	AREA OF RESPONSIBILITY	HEADQUARTERS
No. 4	Captain H. F. Dubuis	Birkenhead, St. Omer Road. Tel.: 1755.	Stoke Ward, River Wey inclusive, Abbotswood exclusive.	Guildfordians Pavilion Stoke Park. Tel.: 3959.
No. 5	Captain R. W. Black	Daphne Cottage, Orchard Road, Burpham. Tel.: 3221.	Abbotswood inclusive, Burpham, Epsom Railway inclusive.	Green Man, Burpham. Tel.: 1160.
Nos. 6 and 7	Mr. E. H. Shepard	Long Meadow, Longdown Road, Tel.: 1607	Merrow and Downs, Borough Boundary, Halfpenny Lane inclusive.	Whiteways, White Lane. Tel.: 52

"C" Company

COMPANY COMMANDER: Lieut.-Colonel H. C. Theobald, D.S.O., Castleton, Warwicks Bench Road, Guildford. Tel.: 1269.

SECOND-IN-COMMAND: Mr. W. J. Walters, Chantry Dene, Fort Road, Guildford. Tel.: 3908.

PLATOON	COMMANDER	ADDRESS	AREA OF RESPONSIBILITY	HEADQUARTERS
No. 8	Mr. W. J. Walters	As above.	Pewley Downs, Chantries exclusive.	Chantry Dene, Fort Road. Tel.: 3908.
No. 9	Mr. W. B. Thorpe	High Barton, Chantry View Road. Tel.:	Shalford Flats, The Chantries.	Estirol, Pilgrim's Way. Tel.: 104

"D" Company

COMPANY COMMANDER: Captain C. H. Frisby, V.C., Glenwoods, Guildown Road. Tel.: 482.
SECOND-IN-COMMAND: Captain G. L. Bartrum, Brambletye, Guildown Road. Tel.: 640.

PLATOON	COMMANDER	ADDRESS	AREA OF RESPONSIBILITY	HEADQUARTERS
No. 10	Captain G. L. Bartrum	As above.	Guildown, Reservoir and Farnham Road inclusive.	Henley Grove Fort Tel.: 746.
No. 11	Mr. C. S. How	Sunnydown, Hog's Back. Tel.: 178.	Hog's Back, Old and New Borough Boundary to Reading Railway line. Farnham Road inclusive.	Sunnydown. Tel.: 178.
No. 12	Mr. W. G. Shephard	Bethwynd, Ridgemount, Guildford. Tel.: 821 (day) Tel.: 428 (night)	Onslow Ward, Stag Hill, Borough Boundary Reading line inclusive.	Guildford Park Farm.

APPENDIX "B"

ROLL OF OFFICERS, 4TH (GUILDFORD) BATTALION SURREY HOME GUARD

Battalion Headquarters: Lea Pale Lane Barracks.

GUILDFORD NODAL POINT.
3rd December, 1944.

COMMANDING OFFICER: Lieut.-Colonel G. W. Geddes, D.S.O., O.B.E.
SECOND-IN-COMMAND: Major C. H. Frisby, V.C.
INTELLIGENCE OFFICER: Captain A. M. Smith.
AMMUNITION OFFICER: Captain G. C. Vincent.
ASSISTANT AMMUNITION OFFICER: 2/Lieut. H. S. E. Flint.
TRANSPORT OFFICER: Lieut. R. C. Jennings.
ASSISTANT TRANSPORT OFFICER: 2/Lieut. C. W. Levinge.
MEDICAL OFFICER: Major G. H. Hollis.
REGULAR OFFICERS ATTACHED: Captain R. P. Turgel (Adjutant).
Captain A. Forbes (Quartermaster).

GENERAL DUTY COMPANIES

No. 1 SECTOR.
Battle Headquarters:
Football Pavilion, Joseph's Road.

"A" COMPANY.

COMPANY COMMANDER: Major A. D. Crosby, M.B.E.
SECOND-IN-COMMAND: Captain A. Light.

Lieut. D. J. Morris.   Lieut. C. H. Brown.
Lieut. S. J. Pigott.   Lieut. L. Barton.

No. 2 Sector.
Battle Headquarters:
Old Farm, Nightingale Road.

No. 3 Sector.
Battle Headquarters:
25, Harvey Road.

No. 4 Sector.
Battle Headquarters:
Pewley Fort.

General Reserve.
Battle Headquarters:
Sandfield Schools.

"B" Company.

Company Commander: Major R. W. Black.
Second-in-Command: Captain C. E. Lord.
Lieut. A. D. Coward.   2/Lieut. J. McCraken.
Lieut. S. G. Higlett.   2/Lieut. J. F. Tilden.

"C" Company.

Company Commander: Major C. R. Wigan, M.C., T.D., D.L.
Second-in-Command: Captain E. H. Shepard, M.C.
Lieut. H. R. S. Law, V.D.   Lieut. W. G. Wright.
Lieut. E. P. Cotton.   2/Lieut. P. Towle.
Lieut. P. Long.

"D" Company.

Company Commander: Major M. Bevan.
Second-in-Command: Captain E. B. Nicklin.
Lieut. A. M. Lester.   Lieut. G. H. Penney.
Lieut. J. C. Stevens.   2/Lieut. D. E. Tyrrell.
Lieut. S. C. Vincent.

"E" Company.

Company Commander: Major P. J. Spooner.
Second-in-Command: Captain H. King.
Lieut. N. B. Harris., M.M.   Lieut. C. F. J. Swain.
Lieut. W. J. Jaquis.   2/Lieut. C. D. Baker.

No. 5 Sector.
Battle Headquarters:
St. Saviour's Hall.

Headquarters:
(a) Dennis Bros.
(b) General Reserve.

"F" Company.

Company Commander: Major O. Crawt.
Second-in-Command: Captain H. W. Gullick and Captain R. P. Slaughter.
Lieut. R. T. Gates. 2/Lieut. F. A. Lingwood.
Lieut. W. T. Smith. 2/Lieut. H. Shanks.
Lieut. F. H. Tucker. 2/Lieut. N. D. Skinner.
Lieut. F. Wingham. 2/Lieut. D. R. Thomas.
Lieut. A. P. Carrington.

FACTORY UNITS

"G" Company.

Company Commander: Major C. T. Skipper.
Second-in-Command: Captain E. T. Clarke, D.S.M.
Dennis Bros. Borough Electricity Dept.
Lieut. R. W. Arnold. Lieut. W. F. May.
Lieut. L. Tallant.
Lieut. R. Wiseman.
R.E.M.E. P.A.M.
Lieut. L. H. McPherson. 2/Lieut. J. A. Ringway.

APPENDIX "C"

THE DISPOSITION, STRENGTH AND WEAPONS OF THE BATTALION. GUILDFORD NODAL POINT

"A" Company—*No. 1 Sector*

Locality	Garrison Strength	Team Weapons M.G.	Team Weapons Smith	Team Weapons S.M.	Personal Weapons	Remarks	
1	22	1	1	1	10	(a) M.G. found by "F" Company	
4	22	1	1	1	10	Ditto.	
8	12	1	1	1		(b) Paper strength, *less* 20%	288
7	20	1	2	1		(c) Garrison 156⎫	
6	32	1		1	20	(d) Battle Sections 60⎬	288
9	10				10	(e) Reserve ... 72⎭	
10	18	1		1	10	(f) 36 (Football Ground).	
						36 (Stoke Mansion).	
11	16	2	2				

"B" Company—*No. 2 Sector*

Locality	Garrison Strength	M.G.	Smith	S.M.	Personal Weapons	Remarks	
13	20	2	2			Paper strength, *less* 20%	176
14	14				10	Garrisons 104⎫	
15	4			1		Battle Sections 30⎬	176
16	9			1	5	Reserve ... ... 42⎭	
17	38		1	1	30	One Boys A/T. locality	17
18	19			1	15		

"C" Company—*No. 3 Sector*

Locality	Garrison Strength	M.G.	Smith	S.M.	Personal Weapons	Remarks	
19	23		1	1	15		
20	15				15	One Boys A/T. locality	20
21	4		1				
22	19			1	15		
23	18		1	1	10		
24	18	1			10	M.G., S.M. and teams found by "D" Company.	
						Paper strength, *less* 20% ...	151
						Garrisons 89⎫	
						Battle Sections 30⎬	151
						Reserve 32⎭	

"D" Company—*No. 4 Sector*

Locality	Garrison Strength	M.G.	Smith	S.M.	Personal Weapons	Remarks	
24	8	1	1	1		Paper strength, *less* 20%	188
25	26	1	1	2	10	Garrisons 102⎫	
26	15				15	Battle Sections 50⎬	188
27	10				10	Reserve 36⎭	
28	29			1	25		
29	14			1	10	One Boys A/T. locality	27

"F" Company—*No. 5 Sector*

Locality	Garrison Strength	M.G.	Smith	S.M.	Personal Weapons	Remarks
30	18	1B	1		10	Take over Browning M.G. from "D" Company.
31	14	1V			10	Take over Vickers from "D" Company.
32	28	1B		1	20	
33 } 34	28		1	1	20	Paper strength, *less* 20% ... 350
35	24				20	Garrisons 203 ⎫
36	15				15	Battle Sections 100 ⎬ 350
37 } 38	35	LP	TP		35	Reserve 47 ⎭
39	46	1V	1	2	30	(*a*) 27 (Cricket Pavilion.) (*b*) 20 (St. Mary's Area.)
40 ×	28	Electricity			28	? Southern Railway and two Lewis.
41A } 41	22		1	2	10	
1	4	1V				×Garrison by "A" Company, *less*
4	4	1V				× M.Gs. Two Boys A/T. Locality 35.

GENERAL RESERVE "E" COMPANY, SANDFIELD SCHOOLS

"G" Company—*Dennis Bros.*

APPENDIX "D"
AWARDS FOR MERITORIOUS SERVICE

O.B.E.
Lieut.-Colonel G. W. Geddes, D.S.O.

M.B.E.
Major A. D. Crosby.

B.E.M.
Sergt. H. Norton, "F" Company.

Certificate of Merit

Sergt. H. W. Collins	"A" Company.
Sergt. H. Court	"B" Company.
C.S.M. H. R. Warren	"C" Company.
Pte. E. Colebrook	"D" Company.
Cpl. J. A. Stowell	"E" Company.
Pte. W. J. Davies	"E" Company.
C.Q.M.S. R. Bullen	"F" Company.

www.ingramcontent.com/pod-product-compliance
Lightning Source LLC
Chambersburg PA
CBHW061419090426
42743CB00027B/3500